The Chinese Palace at Oranienbaum

Catherine the Great's Private Passion

To my mother and father

First published in 2003 by Bunker Hill Publishing Inc
26 Adams Street, Charlestown, MA 02129 USA
6 The Colonnade, Rye Road, Hawkhurst, Kent TN18 4ES UK

10 9 8 7 6 5 4 3 2 1

Library of Congress Cataloging in Publication Data available from the publisher's office

ISBN 1 59373 001 2

Designed by Louise Millar

Printed in China by Jade Productions

Endpapers: Detail of the decoration in the Minor Chinese Cabinet

Opposite : The Exterior and Entrance Hall of the Chinese Palace showing an 18th century copy of Apollo Belvedere.

The Chinese Palace at Oranienbaum

Catherine the Great's Private Passion

WILL BLACK

BUNKER HILL PUBLISHING

BOSTON • LONDON

WORLD MONUMENTS FUND®

World Monuments Fund (WMF) is the foremost private, non-profit organization dedicated to preserving imperilled works of art and architecture worldwide. Since its founding in 1965, WMF has worked with local communities and partners to stem the loss of more than 400 important sites in 80 countries, including such iconic monuments as Angkor, Petra, and the Valley of the Kings, through fieldwork, advocacy, grant-making, education, and training.

WMF in Britain is engaged in projects in the UK and Russia, where it has just completed a project on Yelagin Island, St. Petersburg and is currently co-ordinating the Chinese Palace international appeal with a $3 million target.

World Monuments Fund in Britain
2 Grosvenor Gardens, London SW1W 0DH
Tel: 00 44 20 7730 5344   Fax: 00 44 20 7730 5355
E-mail: will@wmf.org.uk   Website: www.wmf.org.uk

World Monuments Fund (US)
95 Madison Avenue, 9th floor, New York, NY 10016
Tel: 001 646 424 9594 Fax: 001 646 424 9593
Website: www.wmf.org

The State Museum-Estate of Oranienbaum
48 Dvortsovy prospect, 189519 Lomonsov, St. Petersburg

The Menshikov Palace, Japanese Pavilion, Palace of Peter III and Chinese Palace are open 10am-5pm. Closed Tuesdays. The Chinese Palace is closed during the winter months. Restoration is ongoing throughout the estate, and you would be advised to check the opening times of the Chinese Palace with the museum on (007 812) 422 3753 or 422 4796.

The enduring sweep of the Neva and the facade of Hermitage and Winter Palace backed by the gold dome of St. Isaac's cathedral still form the skyline of St. Petersburg.

Introduction

The Chinese Palace, the most important building on the Oranienbaum estate today, was built in the first six years of Catherine's reign, when this politically brilliant, intellectually gifted woman of great courage and intelligence had to work hard to establish her legitimacy: after all, she had overthrown the rightful emperor, her husband Peter III. Its splendor was part of this effort to charm and dazzle Europe.

Her great companion of these years, her lover, was Grigory Orlov, the bluff and handsome Guards officer who had helped her seize power. Orlov supposedly possessed the face of an angel with the body of a warrior, but, more than anything, Catherine needed allies within the Praetorian Guard of St. Petersburg, which could make and destroy emperors. The Orlov brothers were all said to be giants: they provided the 'muscle' that Catherine would need to protect her and ultimately to seize power. Orlov's brother Alexei, also known as "Scarface", possessed the political ruthlessness that the hearty Grigory did not.

Together the three set up the coup d'état. Following its success, the Orlovs were rewarded with lavish gifts and the title of count. Catherine could not have taken power without them and she never forgot the debt she owed them.

Grigory Orlov was not merely a jolly ruffian: he tried to share Catherine's hobbies, he corresponded with the philosophers, built beautiful palaces, and collected fine paintings and jewels. Yet he did not become her first minister. He was too lazy and perhaps not clever enough to conduct policy or run the bureaucracy, though she placed him in charge of southern territories and the artillery. She seems to have realized his limitations, and she would not agree to marry him, which frustrated the Orlov brothers' highest aspirations.

Nonetheless, Catherine shared all her artistic interests with Orlov, particularly in architecture, and this spectacular and exquisite jewel of a palace would have been a joint project with him. It stands today partly as a historical monument, partly as an object of great beauty and artistry, partly as a showpiece of Catherinian imperial ambition, but partly too as a symbol and a venue of the special romance and partnership of Catherine and Orlov. Together they would have visited it and discussed its building, décor, and

Reflected in the ornamental lake, the exterior of the Chinese Palace

A miniature of Grigory Orlov, Catherine's lover and co-conspirator. 'A hero…like the Ancient romans…. and is of just such bravery and magnanimity…. ' as Catherine herself said.

gardens. We know it was first used in 1768, when it was not yet fully finished.

Catherine always longed for stability and claimed she would have been happy to be with Orlov forever, but his infidelities and debaucheries became notorious. In 1772, Catherine's relationship with Orlov collapsed, probably as she began to notice the other great love of her life: Potemkin, who was also physically described as a giant and famed for his good looks, recently marred by the loss of an eye. The Orlovs hated him and may even have beaten him up, allegedly leading to the loss of the eye, but this seems unlikely. They called Potemkin "Cyclops" anyway. However, Potemkin was much more fascinating than Orlov, an astute politician, a political dreamer, a master of executing vast schemes, a beguiling talker, supremely cultured and intelligent, a builder of great cities and conqueror of the Crimea and south Ukraine, a colossus who was one of the most extraordinary men ever to play a great role in the history of Europe.

In the early 1770s, Orlov was raised to prince and sent traveling. By the time he returned he was ill, suffering perhaps from mental imbalance, which may have been syphilitic insanity; he died soon afterward. Prince Potemkin, whom Catherine probably did secretly marry, remained the empress's partner in power until his death in 1791.

Young Grand Duchess Catherine Alexeevna, by Virgilius Eriksen, 1750's

7

This book will introduce the reader to one of the most vibrant and inspiring historic sites in Russia today at a time of crisis. Catherine's Chinese Palace is steadily being eaten away by rising damp, which is destroying the original interiors, and urgent rescue methods are needed. The Chinese Palace has come down to us today, having endured the Revolution, Stalin, Hitler, the stagnation of later Soviet years, and the neglect of the early 1990s and has for too long been abandoned and ignored.

The mission to save it is one of the most important cultural projects not just in Russia, but in Europe. For that reason we should all be heartened by the World Monuments Fund's initiative to rescue this vivid piece of Catherine's life. A major fundraising appeal is under way, and the race to raise funds, as well as international awareness, in which this book will play an important role, has begun.

SIMON SEBAG MONTEFIORE

Second storey of the Chinese Palace, where the effects of time and water damage have clearly taken their toll.

East wing, where only a fragment of the original gardens survives.

Private Passions –
The Chinese Palace of Catherine the Great at Oranienbaum

No other palace in Russia retains so loyally the spirit of its owner as Catherine the Great's Chinese Palace at Oranienbaum. It is easy to imagine her wandering freely through the intimate rooms of her summer dacha, with its secluded setting, and its rococo-style depictions of the muses, art, and love, and images of Catherine herself. It was she who bucked the trend of the estate's previous owners, who had met their demise at Oranienbaum, the "palace of vicissitudes" that had always retained the unhappy atmosphere of past events in its contrasts of great beauty and brutality. Catherine was unafraid of these ghosts, and unlike the rest of the estate, her "personal dacha" remains a testament to her acquisition of power and the more agreeable times that followed her coup d'état.

It was the first palace she commissioned in her reign, and it exudes her personal tastes. This was not a palace she built for the court or for business, but for herself, and for card games and relaxing in private. Often this would have been in the company of her co-conspirator and lover, Grigory Orlov, and the palace is perfect for an afternoon tryst or the pursuit of solitude.

Oranienbaum also has a resonance after Catherine's time. In Yevgeny Zamyatin's futuristic novel *We*, the narrator escapes his controlled, 1984-type environment to spend illicit time with a woman in a palace museum whose description is thought to match that of the Chinese Palace. Written in the 1920s, Zamyatin's book was the first anti-utopian novel ever written, and a warning against the dangers of unquestioned authority. The book was not published in the Soviet Union under Stalin, and Zamyatin escaped the country in 1931.

During the Second World War, the retreating Germans forces destroyed most of the Imperial countryside residences surrounding St. Petersburg, in a futile act of revenge. But the Chinese Palace was untouched, so it has special significance because of the survival of its original interiors. After the war, the palaces at Peterhof and Tsarskoe Selo were valiantly reconstructed and photographs of their destruction are on display throughout. Overtaken by 20th Century history, these reconstructed palaces stand as much as symbols of national pride following the Second World War, as former royal residences.

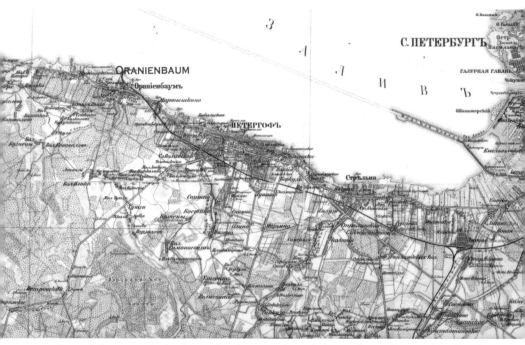

Pre-revolutionary map showing the coastal road to Oranienbaum, leading South West of St. Petersburg along the Gulf of Finland. Containing the estates (from left) of Oranienbaum, Peterhof and Strelna, Catherine rode this route into St.Petersburg to seize power.

In terms of style and scale, the Chinese Palace provides a more intimate experience for today's visitor than those grandiose set pieces at Peterhof and Tsarskoe Selo, overwhelming in their repetitive formal baroque style, which served to extol the power of the czarina rather than her character.

Visiting the Chinese Palace, one simply seems to be breathing in the eighteenth century, an immediate experience no other place in Russia, or indeed Europe, provides.

12

1. Beauty and Brutality—
the History of Oranienbaum

The estate of Oranienbaum has a remarkable history stretching back beyond that of Catherine. The arrest and murder of her husband, Peter III, seems to be a chilling throwback to the downfall of the man who gave his name to the main palace at Oranienbaum, Prince Alexander Menshikov.

Alexander Menshikov, the favorite and, as recently suggested, lover of Peter the Great, fell from grace in 1728, when he was stripped of all of his titles and estates and banished to Siberia. Menshikov, for a time the richest man in Russia, had lived extravagantly, building palaces in the new capital of St. Petersburg and in the suburbs. These were even more magnificent than those of the czar, who had promoted him as their friendship flourished. The crown jewel of his collection of estates was Oranienbaum, built on recently conquered lands in a gesture to please his mentor Peter.

The Grand Staircase leading up to the Menshikov Palace.

Church at the Western end of the Menshikov Palace enfilade.

Original plan for the Chinese Palace with gardens and pond, 1796. (K. Antonii after Rinaldi's drawing)

Oranienbaum was the grandest baroque palatial complex to be built in Russia during the 18th century. In German oranienbaum means "orange tree," a symbol of everything that was scarce, luxurious, and only available to the aristocracy. Oranienbaum began life at about the same time as Peterhof, Peter the Great's maritime residence, from which it is 5 miles (8 km) west. In 1710 construction began on the main palace under the direction of Giovanni Fontana, an Italian architect working with many other European architects under Peter the Great. Fontana also built another lavish palace for Menshikov in the center of St. Petersburg.

In 1737, with Menshikov long departed, Oranienbaum was taken over by the state. In 1743 Empress Elizabeth presented it to her nephew, Grand Duke Peter (later Peter III), and arranged his marriage to Catherine (later Catherine the Great) in August 1745, when Catherine was merely 16 years old.

All that remains of Peter III's miniature military fortifications, the Honorary Gate built by Antonio Rinaldi in 1757.

At Peter's request, the architect Antonio Rinaldi began work at Oranienbaum in 1756, and continued there for 10 years. Rinaldi, born in Italy in 1709, was originally invited to the Ukraine by Count Kyril Razumovsky in 1752, and worked for him at Kiev and Baturin. Kyril was the younger brother of Elizabeth I's morganatic husband Alexei, and so ensured that Rinaldi would become the first court architect, not just for Peter III, but also later for Catherine herself.

Rinaldi started at Oranienbaum with some alterations to the Menshikov Palace before constructing a new, perfectly square, miniature palace (the Palace of Peter III) in rococo style. Military parades and even toy soldiers obsessed Peter III, so his palace was furnished with small-scale fortifications.

Peter III was not a strong ruler and his reputation has been demolished by history, a tradition started by Catherine herself. During his six-month reign he in fact introduced some radical reforms, such as abolishing the secret police. Peter had spent the first 14 years of his life in Holstein and his reluctant relocation to Russia was due to the intrigues of his aunt Elizabeth. Peter retained his admiration for Frederick the Great by adopting the German style of dress for himself and his soldiers, which in Russia was viewed as unpatriotic. Upon his accession on December 25, 1761, he concluded the war against Germany with a peace that was extremely disadvantageous to Russia. By his own actions and, when possible, the interventions of his wife, he became increasingly unpopular in Russia. Catherine meanwhile, although also German, possessed an affinity for Russia that she could turn to her advantage.

1762 was the decisive year in Russian imperial history. By now, Peter III had for many years been antagonistic and difficult toward Catherine—so much so that in the summer, he wished to marry his mistress Elizabeth Vorontsov. He gave an order for his wife Catherine's arrest, which had to be retracted by his uncle Prince George. Catherine felt that the only way to ensure her own survival was to seize power, so she assembled a band of supporters, who would be loyal to her above the ruling czar.

On June 27, 1762, Catherine's hand was forced by the arrest of one of her co-conspirators, Captain Passek, following false rumors of her own arrest.

Catherine's plot was carried out the next day, on the morning of June 28, after she was woken by Alexei Orlov and informed of Passek's arrest. While Peter lay hungover in bed in his small palace at Oranienbaum, Catherine raced from Peterhof to St.

17

Portrait of Grand Duke Peter Fedorovich, Later Emperor Peter III, by Fedor Rokotov, 1758.

Petersburg to gather political and military forces around her. Despite the risks, she received an enthusiastic reception at her inspection of the troops at the new Winter Palace: "The instant I appeared, the air was rent with shouts of joy."

At about 10 o'clock at night, Catherine changed into the green uniform of the Preobrazhensky Guards and prepared to march back to arrest her husband, who had moved from Oranienbaum to Peterhof, where he was expecting to meet his wife to celebrate the Feast of Sts Peter and Paul. In Mon Plaisir, Peter's worst fears were confirmed with the ghostly sight of his wife's untouched gala dress. Dejected and confused, Peter returned to Oranienbaum and prepared to renounce his empire.

He was arrested by a band of troops headed by Alexei Orlov, brother of Catherine's lover Grigory. Demanding only his dog, his violin, his black servant, and not to be parted from his mistress, he was sent by Catherine to nearby Ropsha. He was refused his mistress, but permitted his other requests. In a highly nervous state and allegedly drinking to excess his pitiful end was short, as just over a week after his arrest, Peter was killed when a fight broke out at Ropsha. Alexei Orlov, who had already referred to Peter as "our freak," throttled him and, if the order was not conveyed overtly, Alexei must have felt he had the Empress's tacit approval for his action. Catherine shed bitter tears, not for husband but for the stain on her reputation. However, Alexei was not punished, the real reason for Peter's death was kept secret and Catherine absolved her guilt thus:

"...In a word, God has bought everything about to his own pleasure, and the whole is more of a miracle then a merely human contrivance, for assuredly nothing but Divine will

June 28th 1762 Catherine the Great, dressed for action in the ancient uniform of the Preobrazhensky Guards, discarding the hated Holstein uniforms, on the way to arrest her husband.

could have produced so many felicitous combinations" Catherine herself said in her letter to Stanislav Poniotowsky, August 2, 1762.

Upon her ascent to the imperial throne, Catherine surprisingly did not abandon Oranienbaum. She used it as her private retreat in her early years and embellished the estate accordingly. She had plans for a garden there and had bought some land adjoining the estate eight years before Peter's murder.

So it was in 1762 that she decided to build a palace that was "hers and hers alone," a secluded setting where she could relax with friends and guests. She commissioned the architect Rinaldi, whose work she was familiar with, to build the Chinese Palace in the latest architectural fashion, the rococo style. Six years later, on July 27, 1768, following a service at the Menshikov Palace, the Chinese Palace opened with a lunch for 42 guests and a tour of the gardens.

19

2. Rococo and the Baroque Explosion –
Architectural Styles in St. Petersburg

The rococo style at Oranienbaum and the Italian architect Antonio Rinaldi were both imported from the West. St. Petersburg had already become something of a testing ground for western European styles as French, German, Italian, and British architects transformed Russia's western point of entry into a European city.

Rococo began as a stylistic ripple in France and swept like a wave through Germany and the rest of Europe before breaking in Russia. Of course, under Catherine, everything had to be bolder, richer, and more impressive. She had to outdo everyone else, and so she would with her Chinese Palace.

Rococo was not a style in its own right, but rather the last phase of the baroque, which was already hugely influential in Russia. Starting back in Italy, Gian Lorenzo Bernini, the creator of the baroque and designer of much of St. Peter's in Rome, transcended the boundaries between architecture and sculpture and used the baroque

with a very specific purpose in mind; to confirm religious belief. Infidels, just by entering the massive church of St. Peter's, were to have true faith revealed to them by the weight of ponderous architectural forms.

In a secular setting, something similar was happening in Russia, with the formal baroque court palaces at Peterhof and Tsarskoe Selo. The power of the czar was God-given, and these palaces were designed to flaunt Russia's wealth and might, as well as confirm the supremacy of the ruling czar.

Tsarskoe Selo is referred to as the "symbol of absolute power," and it is worth remembering Rastrelli's extensive work at Tsarskoe Selo, Peterhof, and Smolny as examples of Petersburg baroque that herald the arrival of rococo in Russia. Between 1749 and 1756 Empress Elizabeth rebuilt Tsarskoe Selo, and while the repetitive forms of the exterior are impressive in their excess, a certain fluidity and lightness to the pilasters emerges, which lack the solid monumentality of high baroque. The effect is

The Catherine Palace at Tsarskoye Selo, a loosening of the traditional baroque formality and the emergence of an architectural style unique to Russia in Rastrelli's masterful façade.

Catherine Palace, main façade detail, showing the caryatids.

cheerful more than overwhelming, and sets the context for Catherine's transition to rococo at Oranienbaum. Indeed, this definitely Russian version of late baroque is occasionally referred to as "Elizabeth's rococo."

Where baroque was dark and ponderous, rococo had a lightness of color and weight. External rococo features had a greater elegance and delicacy, and heavy columns were lightened and replaced by bright abstract decoration. The term for this decoration, which uses shell- or coral-like forms and C and S curves, is *rocaille*. In Germany, at the end of the 17th century, architects such as Dominic Zimmermann used images of birds, animals, trees, and cornucopias as symbols of rococo style. In 1755, Frederick the Great commissioned a Chinese pavilion at Sanssouci, in Potsdam, and Catherine, an admirer of Frederick, was determined to outdo his latest exotic project.

A glimpse through the doorway of the Minor Chinese Cabinet with Oriental inspired wallpaper, gilded portals, and intricate marquetry work.

A Greek head is one of many contemporary statues that decorate the garden

Above all, buildings in rococo style were designed for a completely different purpose than those in baroque. In France and consequently at Oranienbaum, rococo houses were built for the owners' convenience and comfort rather than as ceremonial displays of rank to formal visitors. Catherine also began to separate the architecture of public and private life, in contrast to the behavior of her predecessors.

When Rinaldi created the Chinese Palace, he was creating a warm and intimate setting for Catherine to relax in private. The rococo style is perfect for this. A playfulness is borne out by the internal decoration of rococo, with the introduction of large wall scenes depicting naturalistic flowers, trees, animals, and exotic Chinese motifs.

It is important to remember that the chinoiserie element was based on a European fantasy of the exotic Orient, and another concept imported from the West. Indeed, chinoiserie came to Russia "the long way round," and Catherine would have been aware of the drawings of Sir William Chambers, one of the very few Western architects to have visited China in the 18th century. He published books and engravings in the UK, which spread the ideas of chinoiserie through Europe eventually to Russia.

Catherine's dalliance with rococo was a short-lived affair. Her taste for fashion aside, she was eager to move on from Elizabeth's legacy. She went on to embrace a number of styles, from the English neo-Palladianism of the Italian architect Giacomo Quarenghi (Hermitage Theater) to the "return to antiquity," which began in the early 1770s, when the Chinese Palace was barely finished, and which culminated in Charles Cameron's radical work at Tsarskoe Selo (Cameron Gallery and Agate Pavilion) and also at Pavlosk (1782, Temple of Friendship). Catherine cannot be identified with one single architectural style. As with her lovers, she moved on.

3. "Her Majesty's Personal Dacha" -
Inside the Chinese Palace

The charming seclusion that Catherine envisaged is still much in evidence today. Indeed, the Chinese Palace is hidden from view, with no grand, formal approach. First seen across a lake, which reflects the faded red-and-yellow exterior, the palace is in total harmony with its natural setting.

Inside are some of the Europe's most lavish and elegant 18th-century interiors. Rinaldi had gathered a number of the finest European craftsmen working in the 18th century, including Giovanni Tiepolo, the Barrozzi brothers (Guiseppe and Serafino), Marie-Anne Collot (Falconet's assistant - Falconet was the sculptor of St. Petersburg's most famous statue, the representation of Peter the Great as the "Bronze Horseman"), and Stefano Torelli. Rinaldi himself designed the elaborate parquet floors, using many types of wood, including mahogany, ebony, palisander, amaranth and lemon.

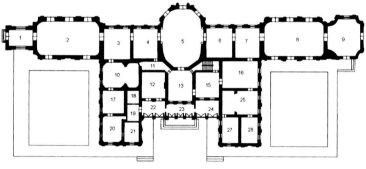

1. Minor Antechamber
2. Major Chinese Study
3. Minor Chinese Study
4. Lilac Lounge
5. Major Lounge
6. Bugle Study
7. Blue Lounge
8. Muses' Lounge
9. Major Antecamera
10 Chinese Bedroom
11. Hallway
12 Heating Equipment Room
13. Entrance Hall
14. Corridor towards 2nd floor
15. Wardrobe Room
16 Pink Lounge
17. Toilet Room
18. Hallway
19 Maintenance Area
20. Portrait Room
21. Catherine II Study
22. Gallery
23. Gallery
24. Gallery
25. Stoph Bedroom
26. Hallway
27. Minor Study
28. Boudoir

Plan of the Chinese Palace, first floor

26 *Lavish but intimate, rococo interiors in the Entrance Hall of the Chinese Palace, with rich parquet and massive wall paintings.*

Twenty-eight rooms make up the ground floor, with nine grand receptions rooms set in an enfilade on the north side. A second level was added to the original one-story building by A. Stakenschneider; court architect in 1848, creator of the Maryinsky Palace and the Little Hermitage, and one of the best-known architects of his time. The palace is long and flat, and not the pagoda style that one finds at the Chinese Pavilion at Sanssouci. Larger than a pavilion, but on the small side for a Russian palace, the building is impressive, yet immediately welcoming.

The modestly named Entrance Hall sets the tone for the whole palace. Lavish scenes painted onto the plaster lend an intense vibrancy that is detailed yet restrained and elegant, complemented by furniture and pictures in keeping with the theme of each room. Indeed, each room is gem on its own, with a logical theme that is carried through in every detail.

The bright and airy Hall of Muses shows the graceful muses in full form, with identifying props, on a background light pinks and blues. Urania, the muse of astrology, is depicted with stars above her head, while Thalia, the muse of comedy, appears at the entrance to the Blue Lounge with a theatrical mask in her hand. Flowers and musical instruments are playfully depicted in the elaborate marquetry. Fifteen types of wood are used throughout the palace parquet to achieve an astonishing variation in color without staining the wood. In this room, used after Catherine's time for concerts, natural light streams in from outside as the French windows seem to melt into the gardens. Throughout the palace, the rococo décor feels like a vine that has crept indoors, merging the outside and inside worlds.

Natural light floods into the Hall of Muses

Thalia, muse of comedy enlivens the Hall of Muses.

The Hall of Muses provides a view of the other suites of rooms, the first of which, the Blue Lounge, depicts scenes of ancient mythology in sensual detail in a large oil painting (Triton and Nereid). The classical themes appear educational, and not just visually stimulating.

One stumbles onto the major attraction of the Chinese Palace even before reaching the central Great Hall. The Glass-Beaded Salon (sometimes called the Bugle Study) is unique in Europe, featuring exotic scenes of birds, cornucopias, and flowers made up of over two million shimmering horizontal glass beads. The effect is breathtaking as the elegant birds glitter in and out of focus. Astonishingly, the room originally contained a glass floor that had to replaced by parquet. The designs are by the Barozzi brothers, and whose production by nine Russian embroiderers was overseen by Marie de Chele, using glass beads from the Lomonosov factory, where they worked from 1762-64. Her signature is on one of the panels, and she was a former actress with a French theatrical troupe at the Russian court. While it is widely believed the entire production was done in Russia, others

Nerida, one of the fifty sea goddesses, section of Triton and Nerida in the Blue Lounge.

Panels of shimmering glass beads in their gilt frames reflect fantasy landscapes in the Glass Beaded Salon.

suggest the scale of the hangings implies the designs might have been done in France and then the glass beads which fill the spaces left by the silk embroidery completed in Russia. Their fragility is apparent, as some of them are starting to unravel. They are fixed to the walls in their gold frames, shaped like palm trunks, so removing them for cleaning would break the threads and shatter these fantasy landscapes. The room also contains two inlaid glass mosaic tables, one showing an ingenious trompe l'oeil game of cards, that were both made especially for the room.

The Great Hall is at the center of the Chinese Palace and dazzles with the richness and variation of its scagliola (decorated or false marble) and unexpected size. In the center was the *Triumph of Mars* by Giambattista Tiepolo, which disappeared after being removed from the ceiling for safekeeping during the Second World War. Busts of Elizabeth Petrovna and her father, Peter the Great, face one another other above each of the doors. Further symbolism is provided by the painting Diana and Endymion, which tells the story of a lowly youth whom a goddess loved. Not only is

Catherine identifying herself with the legitimate imperial dynasty, but with her elevation of Orlov from humble origins.

Finally, one arrives in the two Chinese-style rooms that give the palace its name. The Small Chinese Cabinet shows birds adorning rich Chinese silk, while the parquet has Chinese latticework and bowls of flowers. But it is in the next room that Rinaldi gives free reign to his imagination to create an ornate extreme. In the Great Chinese Cabinet, the ceiling painting showing *The Marriage of Europe and Asia* is framed by a riot of Chinese patterns, fronds, and dragons. The walls are an intricate mosaic of 20 different types of wood showing vast imagined Chinese landscapes.

Opposite: Brightly coloured scagliola adorns the Great Hall, with its bust of Peter the Great above the door

Right: Detail of the intricate decoration in the Glass-Beaded Salon

31

The Major Chinese Cabinet - a riot of chinoiserie. The English billiard table was added later.

Rinaldi's original formal landscape for the Chinese Palace was swept away by the tide of fashion and remodeled by Joseph Bush in the mid-19th century; it is perhaps the only disappointment in the palace today. This is a little ironic, as Joseph Bush of Hackney, London, was one of the most influential landscape designers working in Russia. His father, John Bush, had worked on the intricate gardens at the Catherine Palace for the Empress. Rinaldi's 40 wooden Chinese pavilions, miniature labyrinth and enclosed gardens, which perhaps suited this environment better, were replaced by a supposedly English parkscape with dense woods and lakes. However, what detail has been lost is somewhat compensated by the extreme solitude and seclusion of the park today.

Above: Soon after constructing the Chinese Palace Rinaldi designed some of the pavilions in the gardens at Tsarskoye Selo, and the 'Caprice' was built by Catherine the Great in the 1770's.

Left: Statue of Diana by lake

33

4. Melting Away -
The Condition of the Chinese Palace

From the outside, the Chinese Palace today appears rather battered by the passing of time. The yellow-and-red paintwork looks washed out, and in many places, is crumbling off the exterior. The rainwater pipes are dislocated, and, on the ground, the terrace surrounding the palace is shabby and uneven. In addition, the roof is leaking, so water penetrates the palace both from above and through the sides.

But the leaks are a relatively simple problem compared with the real threat to the palace—water from below. Even before Bush brought more water to the estate, the Chinese Palace and the Oranienbaum complex had always suffered from poor drainage. The decorative lake saturates the land around it with water. As it is so flat, the land in the surrounding park creates an attractive setting with wide vistas, but it drains very badly. This is compounded by high rainfall and heavy snow in the winter and low evaporation in the mild northern summer. These factors combine to create

Uneven terraces and flaking plaster disfigures the North facing façade of the Chinese Palace.

Attacked on all sides by water, exterior damage and inside water rises from the ground as dry rot and leaks in from the roof above.

the worst possible conditions for keeping any building dry.

Right back to Rinaldi's day, ground water has always been the major threat to the Chinese Palace. Rinaldi's original drainage ring had to be built 50 feet (15 m) away from the palace simply to allow Catherine's beloved oak trees to grow. The devastating consequences of water are visible not just externally but internally. The ugly progress of rising damp from the floor upward alerts visitors to the slow but steady decline of the palace's condition. On the walls of the Blue Lounge, and in most of the rooms of the palace, the plasterwork has been eroded above the floor. In two of the rooms, rising damp has already reached a level of 5 feet (1.5 m) above floor level.

There is also the damage one can't see, behind and within the artistic features. The damp internal wall surfaces, the air gap between the walls and the panels, and the complete lack of ventilation or heating in winter provide the perfect conditions for damp and dry rot. Worse, the extreme temperature fluctuations of the Russian seasons subject the artwork to a hideous contrast of temperatures.

Overall, the palace is like a sponge sitting in a bowl of water that is continuously being topped up by the elements and water from the lake.

A broken downpipe pours water back into the palace instead of taking water safely away.

During the 20th century some repairs were attempted at the palace, and a new drainage system, a ring much closer to the palace, was added by G. Preis in 1911. Yet neither this drainage system nor Rinaldi's is operational any longer. The museum administration at Oranienbaum has valiantly done what it can with limited funds to strengthen the palace, closing the shutters in winter and stuffing newspaper into gaps under external doors. But these are desperate measures, not a long-term solution.

Unlike the palaces at Tsarskoe Selo and Peterhof, the estate of Oranienbaum has never received more than very basic state funding for restoration. It seems ironic that because it survived with all its original interiors, the Chinese Palace has been passed over in favor of reconstructing the bombed-out Catherine and Peterhof Palaces. Also in contrast to St. Petersburg's more commercially viable museum estates, Oranienbaum has suffered as a result of a constant change in museum leadership, which has hampered any increase in visitor numbers.

Boundaries of the Oranienbaum territory are still to be defined properly, which could leave it exposed to unsympathetic development. Indeed, a bitumen terminal has been proposed at the end of the canal at Oranienbaum, which would devastate the attractive setting and compromise any public access by sea. This must be stopped, and the terminal resited away from the view of the museum.

In January 2003, the World Monuments Fund began emergency repair work to the roof and the drains from the roof. The next task is the drainage. If the two original systems can be resuscitated, and the palace insulated against ground-water invasion, it would be possible for the palace to dry out. Effective climate controls, ventilation, and heating systems are also urgently required.

Of course, this process of changing the internal environment will affect the artwork, and the restoration will be a painstaking task. The Chinese Palace presents its own unique conservation problems, with its incredible variety of artistic mediums.

Finally, to preserve the sensual and intimate atmosphere of the palace, the temptation to over-restore, to make everything look new, must be avoided.

The Chinese Palace is deserted in the extreme cold of winter.

5. Around the Forgotten Estate – *the Park at Oranienbaum*

It is well worth making the journey out to Oranienbaum to see all the delights on the estate, which provide the context to the Chinese Palace. A short walk from the Chinese Palace is the Sledging Pavilion, another Rinaldi creation and a contemporary of the Chinese Palace. The blue-and-white baroque pavilion is said to resemble a wedding cake and is indeed sugary in appearance. Inside the pavilion, most of the original decoration survives, including a wonderful scagliola floor. The Porcelain Study of the pavilion houses an impressive collection of 40 pieces of Meissen porcelain, supported by waves of white plaster that make up the wall decoration. Collected between 1772-5, they depicts naval victories as well as achievements in arts and science.

Yet it is what no longer remains here that most fires the imagination at this pavilion. Stepping off a second-level balcony, one would have found oneself at the top of a

In scaffolding today, the Sledging Pavilion also requires urgent attention. The wooden switchback would have connected to the pavilion balcony.

Catherine's elaborate rollercoaster

wooden switchback rising some 108 feet (33 m) in the air. There one would have prepared to descend the 1/3-mile (532-m) slide on a wooden cart. Crowds would flock to Oranienbaum to enjoy this lighthearted game of young Catherine's court. Inside the pavilion is an architectural model of the switchback, which gives some idea of its vast scale. Outside, the space for the enormous wooden slide still exists, and should it be put back, would certainly draw visitors.

The condition of the pavilion today is shocking. A few years ago it was open to the

Waves of plaster, some in the form of monkeys or sea-gods support the Meisen porcelain inside the Sledging Pavilion.

public, but today the exterior rests on scaffolding and looks like it has been vandalized, such is the damage to the plasterwork. This is a lesson in the dangers of conservation, since restoration started here but ground to a halt halfway through. It is hoped work will resume some time in 2003.

Visible from the modern road and the first building on the estate (1710), the Menshikov Palace (or "Main Palace") is composed of a compact central enfilade flanked on either side by a church and a Japanese pavilion; stretching for 689 feet (210 m) in total. The architect Fontana (and Schädel) wanted to give the palace an illusion of monumentality, which was achieved by placing it on top of an enormous terrace.

Above: The empty meadow where the rollercoster would have stood

Right: The inside of Sledging Pavilion

43

Guests would arrive by boat from the Gulf of Finland, turn into a long canal, and pass through vast formal gardens, one of the first in Russia, before having to climb an imposing staircase to reach the palace. Today none of the original interiors of its 76 rooms survive as at the start of the First World War the Menchikov Palace was used as a military hospital. While it does retain its original exterior, the drainage problem is so serious threat the terraces are sinking, and the Church and Japanese Pavilion at each end are starting the slide off, exposing hideous cracks in the terrace. It is worth noting that many of the most famous architects of the time, including Bartolomeo Rastrelli and Carlo Rossi worked on various reconstructions of this building.

Built by Rinaldi just before the Chinese Palace in 1758, the square Palace of Peter III is in a more stable condition following restoration. This precise and elegant residence in modest dimensions also houses some elements of chinoiserie style, with panels of black Chinese lacquer and paintings on silk. The main reception and dining room houses 58 paintings, all placed together in a continuous tableau. What has been lost is Peter III's miniature fortress, which encircled his square palace. Ramparts made the shape of a twelve-point star with five bastions, which in turn were surrounded by a deep moat. Soldiers' barracks, and all the requirements of 18th-century fortifications were created for Peter's amusement. Earlier in his life, Peter III had ordered an execution ceremony for a rat that had nibbled at one his toy soldiers. Besides the plan for this fortress, the honorary entrance arch, also by Rinaldi, survives.

The miniature square Palace of Peter III

6. After Catherine

Catherine and Orlov drifted apart in the early 1770s, and Orlov certainly had taken other lovers. Catherine claimed she would have stayed with him if "he had not tired of her first." She owed Orlov and his brother her throne. However Orlov's rough-and-ready charms would be no match for those of the companion of her life, Prince Potemkin, who had already caught Catherine's eye. The end of her relationship with Orlov caused Catherine to abandon Oranienbaum and all it stood for in favor of Peterhof and Tsarskoe Selo as her principal country residences. Orlov passed his last unhappy years at Gatchina.

In 1853 A. Shtakenschneider added a second story to the Chinese Palace. The Oranienbaum estate was then acquired privately and lived in by the Mecklenburg-Strelitz family, before being abandoned during the Revolution. The Chinese Palace opened as a museum for the first time in the summer of 1922.

On July 23, 1941, with St. Petersburg facing a German invasion, the palace closed and some of the contents were taken to Novosibirsk and Sarapul by train. The remaining pictures, panels, and glasswork were transported to the Hermitage and St. Isaac's Cathedral by barge along the Gulf of Finland. There they were safe, for as history famously relates, the Germans were never able to take the city of St. Petersburg.

Another twist of fate saved what was abandoned at the site as the Germans never occupied the Oranienbaum area and so never discovered the Chinese Palace. It was reopened on July 7, 1946, and has remained so ever since. In February 1948, the town of Oranienbaum was renamed after the great Russian scientist Mikhail Lomonosov. However, the Oranienbaum estate remained officially closed to foreigners until the late 1980's, due to its proximity to sensitive military sites.

As St. Petersburg celebrates its 300th anniversary in the summer of 2003, it seems the current President may be trying to emulate some of Catherine's knack of extolling Russia's status through architecture. At a cost of over £115 million ($184 million), and at the center of the celebrations,

St. Petersburg, a city of bridges, and a bridge to the West. The River Neva from the Winter Canal.

President Vladimir Putin is reconstructing the Imperial residence of Strelna, all but destroyed in the Second World War, which lies on the same road as Oranienbaum. For the first time since the Tsars, Russia's president will have a maritime residence in St. Petersburg in which to entertain and impress foreign visitors. The Peterhof road, and the estate of Oranienbaum will enjoy an importance that has been missing since the Romanovs.

St. Petersburg is not Russia, and Russia is not totally European, but St. Petersburg is a seductive blend of both, as it has been for centuries. The Chinese Palace has lasted much longer than Rinaldi intended, and survived in an often incredibly hostile environment. It is a survivor of Catherine's time and a highlight of any tour of St. Petersburg. But it is an exotic creature very much on the verge of extinction, now besieged by nature herself. It could be saved.

Further reading and sourced materials

Dmitri Shvidkovsky *St. Petersburg Architecture of the Tsars* (Abbeville Press)

Zoia Belyakova *The Romanov Legacy* (Hazar)

Simon Sebag Montefiore *Prince of Princes – The Life of Potemkin* (Weidenfeld & Nicolson)

V. G. Klementyev *The Chinese Palace at Oranienbaum* Китайский Дворец В Ораниенбауме (Blits)

Professor Lindsey Hughes *Peter the Great - A Biography* (Yale)

George Heard Hamilton *The Art and Architecture of Russia* (Yale)

Zoé Oldenbourg *Catherine the Great* (Heinemann)

S. B. Gorbatenko *Peterhof Road* Петергофская Дорога (European House)

Pavel Mann *The Environs of St. Petersburg* (Bonechi)

A. Margolis *The Museums of St. Petersburg – A Short Guide* (Ego)

Margarita Albedil *Saint Petersburg The Northern Capital of Russia* (Alfa-Color)

Victor and Audrey Kennett *The Palaces of Leningrad* (Thames and Hudson)

Gert Streidt, Klaus Frahm *Potsdam* (Konëmann)

Princess Katya Galitzine, *St. Petersburg: The Hidden Interiors* (Hazar Publishing)

Picture acknowledgements

Cathy Giangrande: Frontispiece, page 6. Brian Curran/Will Black WMF: Back cover (middle), pages 5, 13, 14, 16, 22, 28 (both), 33 (right), 34, 36 (top right) 40, 42 (both), 43 (right), 44, 46. John Stubbs/WMF: Front Cover (main), pages 8, 10 22, 37, 42, 36 (various), 37. Fritz von der Schulenburg (The Interior Archive): Front Cover (top), pages 23, 24,26, 27, 32, 33 (left), 35. N.Karmazin, with thanks to theOranienbaum Museum and Academia Rossica: front cover (bottom), pages 28,29, 30, 38, 41. Courtesy of the State Hermitage Museum, St.Petersburg: pages 7 (Orlov), 19. Courtesy of the Oranienbaum museum: Front cover (middle), pages 7 (Catherine). Courtesy of Sebastian Zinovieff: pages 12, 25, 36 (various). The Tretyakov Gallery, Moscow, Russia. Courtesy "Olga's Gallery"; page 18. Ellen Rooney: page 20. Maureen Cassidy-Geiger: Back cover (top and bottom), page 34. Russian Union of Travel Industry: pages 46, 48

With thanks to

Simon Sebag Montefiore for his fluent introduction and unflagging support of WMF.

Cathy Giangrande and Colin Amery for their encouragement and wit; and Alice Yates, Naomi Gordon and Kevin Rogers at WMF in Britain for their support.

The following provided information or images for this book and have all furthered the cause of the Chinese Palace in some significant way:

Viktor Gribanov and V G Klementyev and all at The Museum-Estate of Oranienbaum, St. Petersburg; Brian Curran; Professor Dmitry Schvidkovsky at the Moscow Institute of Architecture; Sebastian Zinovieff; Marina Apakayeva; The State Hermitage Museum, St. Petersburg; Academia Rossica; Karen Howes and Fritz von der Schulenburg of The Interior Archive; Maureen Cassidy-Geiger; Bonnie Burnham, John Stubbs and Angela Schuster at WMF New York; Professor Lindsey Hughes at SSEES; Tania Illingworth; Marina Malyshkina and Patricia Falk.

Further thanks to Louise Millar for her brilliant design work and Ib Bellew for commissioning the book and making it happen.

Finally, my two brothers and H. Graciet.